Crushed olives, releases fresh oil

"Not just a book, but a testimony"

A testimony to encourage you to go through the full process to get all the oil from you properly, for the purpose of your assignment in the kingdom of God.

Garvin R. Prichett, Sr.

xulon
PRESS

Dedication

I would like to dedicate this testimony, to these people who are apart of my testimony:

To my lovely wife, who stuck by my side during the process of this testimony and who is a prime example of a help meet; Co-Pastor Connie Dolores Prichett.

To my late mother, who dedicated her life to raise me in the fear and admonition of the Lord; Gladys Marie Prichett.

To my late mother in law, who showed me unconditional love; Mable Marie Starks.

To our two children yet at home, for their patience and encouraging words; Kya Sharese Dionne Prichett, 16 years old, and My name sake, Garvin Ray Prichett, Jr., 13 years old

To our older children , for believing in me; Timberlaun "Tina" Turner, for letting me practice on her; Christopher Lee Turner, Ethan Dion Turner and Shaniessa Laquoise Prichett.

Our five beautiful grandchildren; Krishawna Ebony Turner, 12 years old; Lazaie Shamoane Turner, 9 years old; Trenton Devon Turner, 8 years old; Devon O'shay Johnson, 8 years old; Emani A'jahnae Turner, 4 years old.

Acknowledgements

irst things first, God, my friend, my strength, my power and ability to go through this process and complete it uncompromisingly; to my big sister who encouraged me to write a book when I didn't know I had one in me, Camille "Loretta" Hill; to my son in the gospel, Bishop Gary Washington and The Church of the true living God, of Oakland, California;

Tyretta Prichett, (sister)
Sylvana Prichett, (sister)
Pastor Richard & Lorena Treece
Pastor Elika & Valencia Stagg
Pastor Nathaniel & Shonda Smith
Pastor Linnette Parchment of Jamaica
Min. Willie J. Frink (nephew)
Min. Marcus Murchinson
*Mother Johnnie B. Hill
*Mother, Elder Josie Mister
The late mother Ada Jones
The late Pastor Charlotte Davis-Clemons
The late Pastor Harold Clemons
The late Pastor Lela Watley

Pastor Tommy Wofford
Pastor Willie Holland
James and Connie Bradley (olive suppliers)
Wayne Winter
Vickie Beggs
Darrell & Juanita Jones
Stephen & Carlene Logan
Danielle Armstead

I can't forget the honorable family of Ambassadors for Christ International Ministries, of which I am privileged to pastor, I love you and appreciate you for sharing me with the world.

Contents

Chapter one:
   The crushing of the olive 13

Chapter two:
   The crushing place (at Gethsemene) 19

Chapter three:
   Afflicted but anointed 25

Chapter four:
   Keep your lamps lit! 31

Chapter five:
   Bring extra oil (just in case) 37

Chapter six:
   When the oil is released 41
   (what grade is your oil?)

Chapter seven:
   My crushing place (my testimony) 47

Chapter eight:
   The deeper call 57

Chapter nine:
   A walk through the dark valley 61

Introduction

I remember the time when the spirit of the Lord spoke to my spirit about writing this book for a testimony for the world, it started with a series He told me to do for the ministry, it was about three years ago, when the Lord impressed on me to study about the process of the crushing of the olive and He told me to title the series, "Crushed olives, releases fresh oil," "anointing"

I prepared a three part series to minister at Ambassadors for Christ, each series titled as followed; "Keep your lamps lit," "Wild olive tree," and Afflicted but Anointed." This series was a great impact on the ministry as well as myself, from there the Lord impressed me to write my testimony in book form, not realizing that saying yes to do so, would take me to a place I never expected to go to.

Ambassadors for Christ Int'l Ministries, the ministry I founded, at this writing now in existence for eight years. During the time God spoke to me to write this book, the ministry would go through a series of splits and would endure some hard demonic attacks, we were hit financially, the membership went from approximately five hundred to under one hundred, we even had to down size in many areas of the ministry, this effected everyone involved, many times

I thought that we were going backwards instead of forward, and often I wanted to closed the door of the ministry and return to the secular work field, but God would speak to me to inform me that this is all part of the plan for the testimony that I was writing for the book that would be birth out of me, you see some of the things that had to take place was to get all the pulpy mass out of the ministry, to receive the pure, fresh oil out of it, for the purpose of the clear oil to light the candles of Ambassadors for Christ, so that it will be as effective as God meant for it to be. God just wouldn't allow A.F.C.I.M. to be just another ministry functioning, not to say that this ministry is better than any other ministry, but that it must be a very effective ministry, a ministry not just with a mission, but on a mission, and a lot a people that was attending the ministry at the time God did not send, so he had to crush the olive of Ambassadors for Christ, to strain and separate the pulpy mass from the clear, pure oil; God was trying the pure motives of those who said that God sent them to A.F.C.I.M.

A.F.C.I.M. went through about three major splits, three crushing of the olive of this ministry, but God gave us the grace to endure hardness as good soldiers.

I am proud to report that we are more than conquers, this ministry is more powerful than it has ever been, God is sending in great men and women alike who have come with a testimony of what process they had to go through to get to us. Prepare to be impacted and ministered to when you read this testimony, you have been waiting on this book, now that it has arrived, cherish it and share it with others that you know need it for such a time as this. The world need that fresh, clear and pure oil to be released from you, so get ready to go all the way through the crushing process, I am praying for you.

Chapter one

The crushing of the olive

*G*od spoke to Moses to command the children of Israel to "bring thee pure oil, olive beaten for the light," Exodus 27: 20. For the oil of the eternal light, to be put in the Tabernacle of the congregation to cause the light to burn always. The people was commanded to bring oil already prepared to light the temple, olive beaten for the light. God is looking to receive eternal light out of His people.

Beaten olive oil was made by bruising the olives in a mortar or mill without heat, or when the olives fell from the tree, it was to go through a process of crushing four times before going to the mortar or mill. This is to get the effects of clear, fresh oil.

The process was by bruising and crushing the olive and straining the olive to get rid of all the pulpy mass and allow the fresh clear oil to be released from each pressure applied to the olive. Each time the substance would be put in a cloth like strainer to strain the pulpy mass or pomace and receive the oil. This would be done repeatedly, to get clearer and purer oil. The substance of the pomace, essentially consist of the pulp of the fruit of the olive, water or other juice that had been pressed out, this also includes the peel, seeds and stalks.

Olive trees and olive plants are symbols of God's people, He speaks of this in His word many times. One occasion King David refers to himself as a "green olive tree in the house of God," you will find this Psalms 52:8,9. In contrast between David and Doeg, David compares the blessings of the just, by trusting in the mercy of God, than that of Doeg who trusted in riches:

"But I am like a green olive tree in the house of God: I trust in the mercy of God for ever and ever. I will praise thee forever, because thou hast done it: and I will wait on thy name; for it is good before the saints." David was like a green olive tree in God's house; Doeg like a dead tree cast out. David trusted in the mercy of God; Doeg trust in riches. David will be blessed forever; Doeg will be cursed forever. David will praise God forever because of God's help; Doeg will live in remorse forever. David waited on God's name; Doeg did not. David was a good example for God's saints; Doeg was an example of evil, by the way, Doeg means fearful, this is what happens when we don't go through the process of waiting and trusting in the mercy of God, it will often lead to fearfulness and having the spirit of fear will eventually curse you forever.

In this Psalm of David, Doeg who had much but wanted more from his treachery of David, went and told lies to King Saul on David to ruin him by slandering his name, sounds familiar? Well, this would be the test of David's faith in the God he is waiting on, you see one of the olives from David's tree is being crushed to receive the fresh clear oil for his next season, he is on his way to the throne, and even though he is anointed to be king, God has to process him out to get it out. Although this treacherous Doeg is slandering his name; David continues to praise God and wait on Him, he never stops trusting God. God sometimes finds it necessary to send a fearful lying Doeg your way to apply pressure on you to attempt to frustrate your purpose, but what the devil meant to stop you, God's purpose in it is to get the fresh, clear oil released from you so that you can see what He has anointed you with. The ones who are lying on you really are fearful of you. Notice the 6 fold character of Doeg:

1. Boastful and treacherous;
2. A liar and a slanderer;
3. A deceiver of personal gain;
4. A lover of evil more than good;
5. A lover of lies more than truth;
6. A lover of seeing others hurt.

There are people around you who are intimidated of your anointing, they themselves are afraid to press into the things of God by trusting Him like you are doing, and I have found out that one reason that people don't obey God is mainly because of the fear of what others are going to say about them, so they rather join the others who are fearful of you and slander your name. I want to encourage you to go through the process of your crushing, it is not designed to kill you, but to heal you, the oil that is invested in you will first heal you, then when you bring your pure, fresh, clear oil to the Lord, for His purpose, after you have been beaten for the light, then others will find their way to you, and that oil will help effectively heal others who was hurting like you.

It is a must that we bring pure oil already beaten and processed for the light, it is that anointing that destroys yokes, God is not soliciting more talents for such a time as this, He is searching for that yielded olive, that is willing to be pressed, beaten, and crushed to receive what is needed for the job.

When the olives fell from the tree, it was to go through a process of crushing four times before going to a mortar or mill. Sometimes God will allow us to go through a process repeatedly before He will accept the oil, a lot of times we want to rush out of what we're going through, because we are embarrassed, we have preached to others on what God is doing and will do, but here you are still in trouble, and at times we feel cursed or maybe we didn't hear from God, but could it be that He is not satisfied with the oil that has already been released, and He is saying go back through the mill again until your motives are 100% pure. The Lord spoke to me one hot early summer morning, when I was walking and praying over my city, in downtown Bakersfield, California, He said, I am not ready to bring you out to the public, because I want to make sure that you don't come out like many of the other men and women of God, before I released them to the world, they stayed on their face before me, they didn't mind being crushed, but the moment I released them, they became arrogant, self centered and prideful, and they used that time to fight back at those who supposedly hurt them before that got to their destiny. The Lord tells me That he won't let me go out that way. I had to go through some more crushing, He said he was keeping me for a particular time and that my motives must be 100% pure. I want to follow David's pattern in this, "I will trust in the mercy of God forever and ever." There are great blessings in waiting on the God of mercy. Deuteronomy 8:7,8 tells us, "For the Lord thy God bringeth thee into a good land, a land of brooks and water, of fountains and depths that spring out of valleys and hills; A land of wheat and barley, and vines and fig trees and pomegranates; of oil olive and honey;" It is very important that you complete the course that God has put you on, so that God will bring you to this good land of the greatest opportunities.

We must be crushed, bruised and pressed in order to get all of the pulpy mass (old sin nature) out of us by being strained, separate from the pure oil that need to be released for the purpose of the kingdom of God. God want to strain the old you out of you, and receive the pure you, no more I, but Christ. Too many of us want the process of change, without the process of pain. We must understand that God creates deeper situations, to create deeper revelations. our vision produces consequences, take a look at Joseph , his vision put him through an intense process, I know there are people in your life and ministry that you expected to support your vision only to find out that they were there until you spoke about making your vision plain, then the opposition began, and this has caused such pain and great loneliness, this position has started the process of change, just don't change positions to fit in, this is the perfect time to develop a real relationship with God and ask him to guide you through this process so that He can complete it in you. God has designed this place for you to go through alone with Him, He has to separate us from certain people so He can get what he needs from inside of us and not from those around us.

With every opportunity, comes opposition. Remember this, "For which cause we faint not; but though our outward man perish, yet the inward man is renewed day by day." 2 Corinthians 4:16. God want you to see what He has produced in you, now He is attempting to get it released from you.

In Leviticus 24:2, where God spoke to Moses to command the children of Israel that they bring unto thee pure oil, olive beaten for the light, to cause the lamps to burn continually in the temple. The lamp in your ministry must be burning continually, no matter who left, or who came, keep burning, that is why it is important for those who are assigned to labor with you in your ministry, they must bring to you fresh oil, not flesh oil. Don't allow people to just come and be counted they must come and be anointed (through the process). Just having a number does not provoke the presence of God. Those that come and say, God sent me to help you in your ministry, I see your vision. You ask for their testimony, not just their resume, their testimony really is their resume. If they can only give you a Greek and Hebrew knowledge, then their first assignment should be a command to go and bring to me pure oil, beaten, clear and pure. In other words you need a testimony from them on what they went through to get to you. Psalms 51:17 says "The sacrifices of God are a broken spirit: a broken and a contrite heart O God, thou will not despise." Two sacrifices are always acceptable:

1. A broken spirit: Hebrew word, "Sha bar" - to shiver, break in pieces, reduce to splinters.
2. A broke and contrite heart: Hebrew word, "Da kah" - to crumble, beat to pieces, bruise, crush, humble, dejected.

These sacrifices are acceptable to God and He does not despise it.

I remember asking God, what was it about me that started the process of him drawing near to me, to begin to commune with my spirit like he did, he simply replied, "You were broken!" my wife puts it this way, "You were raw!" David experienced this when the prophet Nathan came to him after he had sinned with Bathseba, David became broken and had a contrite heart with sorrow for sin and humbly thoroughly penitent. That is why David became a man after God's own heart, why because when he sinned against God or needed help he didn't go after the council of men or the ungodly, but he sought the heart of God with a broken spirit and a contrite heart. If you come to God already fixed up,

what then do you need him to do for you? God fixes broken people, that is why your will has to be broken, so God's will can be developed in you, then released out of you to receive the pure oil for the purpose for the ministry that God has assigned you for.

Chapter two

The crushing place
(The oil press)

The place is called Gethsemane the name is given in the Greek of the Gospels (as Gethsemani), this represents the Aramaic (Gath-Smane), meaning, the oil press or oil vat. It also means the crushing place, The Mount of Olives, was where Judas betrayed Jesus and where Jesus was in agony in the Garden of Gethsemane.

This testimony is found in all four accounts of the Gospels, according to St. Matthew, according to St. Mark, according to St. Luke and according to St. John, we will be taking our text from the testimony according to St. Luke and you will find it in the 22 chapter and 39 verse through 46 verses, Reading from the Amplified version:

And He came out and went, as was His habit, to the Mount of Olives, and the disciples followed Him. And when He came to the place, He said to them, pray that you may not enter into temptation. And He withdrew from them about a stone's throw and knelt down and prayed, saying, Father, if you are willing, remove this cup from me; yet not my will, but (always) yours be done. And there appeared to Him an angel from Heaven, strengthening Him in the spirit. And being in agony (of mind), He prayed (all the) more earnestly and intently, and His sweat became like great clots of blood dropping down upon the ground. And when He got up from prayer, He came to the disciples and found them sleeping from grief, And He said to them, why do you sleep? Get up and pray that you may not enter (at all) into temptation.

The Mount of Olives, was also called Mount Olivet, a mountain ridge to the east of Jerusalem, it is named from the olives trees, with which it's sides are clothed. At the foot of the mountain is the gardens of Gethsemane, where Jesus stayed in Jerusalem and this mount is the site of many biblical events, but not one so meaningful as this particular event, the scene of Jesus' agony and betrayal. Jesus prayed in the gardens of Gethsemane the night before He was crucified. Although Jesus' ministry was successful up to this point, He was to go through a final process of crushing to finish it, so it was necessary that the father sends Him to the oil press for the purpose of the cross. Philippians 4:8, says "And after He had appeared in human form, He abased and humbled himself (still further) and carried His obedience to the extreme of death, even the death of the cross. (amplified)

We must also carry our obedience to the extreme of death, being dead to ourselves, it is important that we don't stop at the success of our ministries, but to the extreme of death, we often speak about being like Christ, after all that is what Christian really means, being Christ like, yes, He paid the ultimate price of going to the cross for our sins, and we won't have to pay that price (thank God), but we must crucify the flesh, Galatians 5:24, makes it plain to us, "And those who belong to Christ Jesus (the Messiah) have crucified the flesh (the godless human nature), with its passions and appetites and desires. (amplified). Every great man and woman of God who ever made and are now making an impact in this world for God, ended up at the crushing place in order to finish their work for the Lord. Jesus took a walk to pray in the garden, where he felt overwhelming sadness and anguish, the disciples following Him, He said to them, in Luke 22:40, Pray that you may not (at all) enter into temptation, and He withdrew from them and knelt down and prayed, saying, Father, if you are willing, remove this cup from me; yet not my will, but (always) yours be done. Luke 22:42. The next verse 43, And there appeared to Him an angel from Heaven, strengthening Him in spirit. While God has you on the oil press, to press the oil out, God will send assistance to help you endure the oil press process, the angel strengthened Him to endure His agony. The ordinary human strength could not have endured the agony. While you are on the oil press, others are wondering how you are able to endure when ordinarily you would have a major breakdown, But God has employed His angel to strengthen you while you are going through, you yourself have asked how are you yet standing through this, the apostle Paul says, "My grace is sufficient for thee: for my strength is made perfect in weakness." Paul's reaction was, "Most gladly therefore will I rather glory in my infirmities, that the power of Christ may rest upon me." Paul learned to glory in his infirmities so that the power of Christ could rest upon him. It is important to learn what it takes to have the power of Christ to rest upon us, you can receive impartation from other anointed men and women of God, someone may even lay hands on you, this power does not rest upon you, to get the power of God to rest upon you, you must be willing to go to your crushing place and stay on the oil press until you have completed the process.

The 44th verse says; And being in an agony (of mind), He prayed (all the) more earnestly and intently, and His sweat became like clots of blood dropping down upon the ground. This crushing place had put Jesus in a very tight position, the bloody sweat, and the terrible struggle in the garden when satan and all his forces sought to kill him before He got to the cross, Hebrews 10:7, Who in the days of His flesh when he had offered up prayers and supplications with strong crying and tears unto him that was able to save him from death, and was heard that he feared. Jesus' sweat blood, means that He sweat his guts out, what agony He endured. It is hard to imagine in the finite mind, of the terribleness of this conflict, but the whole plan of God was at stake, and we must realize the whole plan of God for us, while we're in our crushing place.

If satan could have succeeded here or on previous occasions to kill Christ, he could have averted his own doom and kept control of the earth indefinitely. It was imperative that Christ get to the cross to pay the penalty for sin and conquer satan forever.

I want to encourage you right here, and tell someone who is in their crushing place, that is why you are reading this testimony, because you are trying to make sense out of what you are going through, and you are contemplating either giving up or compromising your purpose just to get some peace, please let me help you now, if you are in the perfect will of God and are not practicing sin and you didn't put yourself in this place, if you are just obeying God and you are here in this crushing place, let me minister to you that it is imperative that you get to your destiny, I understand that it is real tight, and you are under a tremendous amount of pressure, yes there is conflict all around you, but God has dispatched an angel to strengthen you, and prophetic watchmen are praying for you while you endure this process, there are those who depend on you getting to your destiny, it is not just for you, it is for many others, God need that oil for this next season.

The bible said, in the 45th verse that when He arose from prayer, the disciples was sleep for sorrow: And when He arose up from prayer, and was come to His disciples, he found them sleeping for sorrow. Don't be discouraged when those who are following you, don't go with you into the crushing place, after all this place was prepared just for you for the purpose of the call on your life to impact the part of the world that God has assigned you. Everyone cannot go some places where God is taking you to, some are not willing to go through what you are willing to go through for the sake of Christ, you may have an effective staff, and awesome Armour bearer's team, but they can only go so far with you, while you may have to withdraw a stone's throw away from them to experience agony in your crushing place and get on the oil press, and deal with some things that they can't handle right now, so don't become discouraged when they stop to sleep for the sorrow they feel for you.

Agony, what is it? Greek word for agony is agonia, meaning, a struggle, conflict, it is from agon, a place of assembly, especially the place in which Greeks assembled to celebrate solemn games; a place of contest and struggle of exertion to the utmost to overcome all opposition in attaining the goal, hence, it is used of Christians in their fight to spread the gospel among their enemies and live victoriously to the end. It is a recognized fact that under extreme mental pressure, the pores may be so dilated that the blood may issue from them; so that there may be bloody sweat. A number of cases are on record of such agony.

Chapter three

Afflicted but anointed

The fact that Christ suffered affliction proves that it should not be understood as sickness or disease as taught by many. Christ has never been sick, but He has been afflicted. Isaiah tells us in 53: 7, He was oppressed, (yet when) He was afflicted, He was submissive and opened not His mouth; like a lamb that is led to the slaughter, and as a sheep before her shearers is dumb, so He opened not His mouth. He was oppressed and afflicted, yet He opened not His mouth. In Colossians 1:24 Paul states; (Even) now I rejoice in the midst of my sufferings on your behalf. And in my own person I am making up whatever is still lacking and remains to be completed (on our part) of Christ's afflictions, for the sake of His body, which is the church.

Greek gives us several meanings of affliction, one says; "Thlipseos," to crush, press., compress, squeeze, pursue, disturb, agitate, greatly throw into great trouble, vex, annoy and upset.

The pain which is afflicted on you, will either push you down or push you up, and finally push you out. What affliction does is cause constriction, to constrict your space, working in a small constricted space. Your enemy is attempting to constrict your space, to cause anguish from being in a narrow place. It seems like you don't have enough room and it seems to get smaller and you don't have enough time. While your enemy is attacking, God is preparing, to squeeze out and pronounce the blessings from the inside, the improvement of God, (His delight).

Contrary to some teachings, affliction is not a disease or illness, it is temptation usually from an enemy or a test from God. I am not speaking of self affliction, sometimes our afflictions or troubles are situations we got ourselves into, that my friend you will have to ask God to help you, by repenting to Him and move in Jesus name. I am referring to the things that was afflicted on you to squeeze and pronounce the blessings from the inside, the improvements of God, His delight.

David said in Psalms 119:65&66, "Thou hast dealt well with your servant, O Lord, according to your word (promise). Teach me good judgment, wise and right discernment, and knowledge, for I have believed (trusted, relied on, and clung to) your commandments. David makes a thankful acknowledgement of God's gracious dealings with him all along. "Thou hast dealt well with thy servant," God hast dealt well with us, better than we deserve, and all because He loves us and with design to work for our good.

Upon these experiences David grounds a petition for divine instruction: "Teach me good judgment and knowledge." Teach me taste, to discern things that differ, to distinguish between the truth and the lie, good and evil; for the ear tries words, as the mouth tastes meat. Many have knowledge who have little judgment, having great knowledge, but little or no discernment. This is why at times we must be afflicted, to receive the knowledge of who God really is.

Psalms 119:67, David continues, "Before I was afflicted, I went astray, but now I have kept thy word, Here David

tells of the temptation of a prosperous condition: Before I
was afflicted," while I lived in peace and plenty, and knew
no sorrow, I went away from God and my duty. Prosperity
sometimes is the unhappy occasion of much iniquity, if we
don't handle it properly, it makes people conceited of themselves, indulgent of flesh, forget God, love the cares of this
life, and deaf to the reproofs of thy word.

David tells of the benefit of an afflicted state:

"But now have I kept thy word," and so have been
removed from my wanderings. God often makes use of afflictions as a means to reduce those to Himself who wandered
from Him. It is God's way of calling us back to Him, once
we strayed away. In the case of the prodigal sons' distress,
it brought him to himself first, then to his father. Sometimes
God has to bring you down to bring you out, He has to press
down on you, to get all the air out, because we can become
a bit airy at times.

In Psalms 119: 69, David testifies that, "the proud have
forged a lie against me: but I will keep my precepts with my
whole heart." Those that were proud, envied David's reputation because it eclipsed them, in other words, it over shadowed them, that is why people deliberately lie on others to
ruin their reputation of the one who over shadowed them,
they are to proud to acknowledge your position and get with
you because "their heart is fat as grease," now that is what
the bible says, in Psalms 119:69 & 70, the proud are at ease,
their minds are dull and brutal, they are full of the world and
the wealth and pleasure of it. This makes them secure, they
are past feelings, it is the proud people around you who God
will use to afflict you, and attempt to deliver you to himself
and from them. David finally says in verse 71, It is good for
me that I have been afflicted; that I might learn thy statutes,
learn His laws, His established rules, to learn His ways.

The proud and the wicked lived in pomp and pleasure, while David, though he kept close to God and his duty, he was still in affliction.

David could speak with experience, It was good for me to have been afflicted," who is it that would freely speak that it is good to be afflicted, but the one who, not only has knowledge of God but also can discern God, through affliction, David learned many lessons by afflictions. The afflictions had contributed to the improvements of his knowledge and grace. He that chastened him taught him and anointed him.

You must realize that affliction is one of the main contributors to your promise. Sometimes it may take trouble coming your way, so that you may learn more about the ways of Christ and to be established by His rules and not by man's rules only. The more of the anointing, requires more of the afflictions, but remember, trouble won't last always.

Let me make something clear, I don't want you to think that this walk with Christ is only all about suffering and being in pain all the time, but it is necessary for a victorious walk with Christ, affliction does not make a person, it exposes who you really are. You can be called, but still in a crisis, you can be chosen and still be challenged, but you are yet being fruitful in the land of your affliction. Your affliction humbles you, so Christ can exalt you. You will not get beside yourself when you are being challenged by your troubles, because your trust is totally in God almighty, at the height of your anointing, will be the height of your affliction.

Apostle Paul said in second Corinthians 12:7.... "Lest I should be exalted above measure through the abundance of the revelations, there was given to me a thorn in the flesh, the messenger of satan to buffet me, lest I should be exalted above measure."

God did not want Paul to exalt himself (which by the way is so easy to do) through the abundance of the revelations given to him, so he permitted him to have a thorn of flesh to keep him abased and humble.

David was on his way to the throne, while on his way there, he was on the run for 17 years from King Saul, pregnant with a promise, he had a definite divine destiny to be Gods' appointed and anointed King over all of Israel, but Saul was tall and that's all, David was short, ruddy and appointed and anointed, Saul had an army, but David had the anointing, (afflicted but anointed). Affliction is your main contributor to your anointing, anointing brings with it clarity, in order to effectively destroy yokes, you must be anointed, to know where to go to destroy yokes.

But there will come a time in the process, that God will silence the voices that are around you. When you are chosen of God for great plans for you, there will be times He will reduce the noise that is around you, so that you can hear the strong voice of God.

Job 36:15 tells us that, He delivers the afflicted in their affliction and opens their ears (to His voice) in adversity. Be encouraged, although you are afflicted, you are being anointed to hear God's voice in the time of adversity, this is an indicator that you are being equipped with something that only God can equip, while you are on your way to your destiny, you're pregnant with God's promise for greatness, but remember when things get heated up and it seems like your affliction becomes a bit to much for you to handle, this will happen at times, then go to the written word of God, in 1 Chronicles 16:8-22 will come to your rescue, O give thanks to the Lord, call on His name; make known His deeds among the peoples! Sing to Him, sing praises to Him; meditate on and talk about all His wondrous works and devoutly praise them! Glory in His name; let the hearts of those rejoice who seek the Lord! Seek the Lord and His strength; yearn for and seek His face and to be in His presence continually! (Earnestly) remember the marvelous deeds which He has done, His miracles, and the judgment He uttered (as in Egypt), O you offspring of Abraham and of Israel His servants, you children of Jacob, His chosen ones! He is our God; His judgment is in all the earth. (Amplified)

Be mindful of His covenant forever, the promise which He commanded and established to a thousand generations, the covenant which He made with Abraham, and His sworn promise to Isaac.

He confirmed it as a statute to Jacob, and to Israel for an everlasting covenant, saying, to you I will give the land of Canaan, the measured portion of your possession and inheritance.

When they were but a few, even a very few, and only temporary residents and strangers in it, when they went from nation to nation, and from kingdom to another people, He allowed no man to do them wrong; yes, He reproved kings for their sakes, saying touch not my anointed, and do my prophets no harm.

Even though you are being afflicted, yet you are being anointed to go to a great place.

Chapter four

Keep your lamps lit!

*L*eviticus 24:1-4, And the Lord said to Moses, command the Israelites that they bring to you pure oil from beaten olives for the light (of the golden lamp stand) to cause a lamp to burn continually.

Outside the veil of the Testimony (between the Holy and the most Holy places) in the tent of meeting, Aaron shall keep it in order from evening to morning before the Lord continually: it shall be a statute forever throughout your generations.

He shall keep the lamps in order upon the lamp stand of pure gold before the Lord continually.

In every candlestick there should be a burning and shining light; candlesticks without lit candles are like clouds without rain.

Moses commanded the children of Israel to provide the oil (anointing), by the word of the Lord. The priests were responsible for lighting the lamps and to tend them; it is the works of the ministers in your church and city, by the preaching and expounding of the scriptures, to enlighten the church, God's tabernacle on earth.

We have in our churches plenty of trained ministers, who have operated far to long as candlesticks on a lamp stand, without lit candles, little or no anointing, doing ministry with a badge, but carry no gun - power with no authority - they have a mission to minister, but have not waited on the commission from God, they haven't completed the process to go forward.

We have allowed Gods' people to operate in ministry, without commanding from them pure oil already beaten through a completed process, to receive the oil that would keep our ministries constantly and always burning with a shining light; therefore our churches have dim to no light.

The tabernacle of the congregation had no windows, so the lamps were required to be lit during the day as well as every night.

Aaron and his sons were to take charge of the lighting of the lamps with the processed pure oil beaten. They had to use what was given to them from the people, what has been released from the olives when bruised and crushed and without the application of fire.

As I look back during the time of the process of me being crushed when I was evangelizing, God sent me through out the nation to preach the gospel, I was working a fulltime job, had a fulltime family, and while I had these responsibilities, I would at times take off of work without pay, to obey God and travel to where He was sending me, in many places I would have to pay my own way, air fare, hotel expenses, sometimes I had to feed myself with the little money I brought with me, all of this because the church was to small to take care of these expenses, but they needed me to bring some pure oil, already beaten, to assist in lighting the candle of that ministry, often times I would leave without, offering and of course at first I would be pretty discouraged, knowing I had a family to help feed, and I took time off of work, but the Lord, would encourage me that He was taking me through this for a reason, and He was going to prove Himself to me, by sustaining me during time of process, and He did just that, He sustained me and my family and today He has blessed us tremendously.

I remember before I was commissioned to evangelize, the Lord spoke to be by one of His prophets, that He was going to put me on the field first before He would commission me to pastor, so He can show you how to receive evangelists in the church I would pastor, you see I had to keep my lamp lit, by going through a crushing season, serving under five pastors, remaining submissive to them, and as I traveled the nation, I wasn't always treated with respect as I thought I should, sometimes after the Lord would use me to deliver and help a particular ministry, They would send me away wounded and used, but God would always bind the wounds and lift my spirits.

The lamps had to remain lit always, because the tabernacle of the congregation, was the place where God was pleased to reside.

Is God pleased to reside in your ministry?

Before the testimony, that is the ark where the tables of the covenant were deposited.

Aaron and his sons being the only legitimate levitical priests, God having established the priesthood in his family. They shall order it from evening to morning, all seven lamps burned all night: in the morning four were extinguished and three kept burning the entire day.

It is very important that we keep our lamps trimmed and burning always as God's priests on earth.

In Psalms 104:4, God refers to His ministers as "FLAMING FIRE," who makes winds His messengers, flames of fire His ministers. Ministers of the gospel must come with fire,

The Hebrew word for minister is sharath, servants, human ministers of God is the reference, not angels. Almost without exception it is used of the priests and levites of the tabernacle and temple worship and of the servants of Israel's kings - the gospel ministers are successors of the old testament priests.

We are ministers of flame; the Hebrew word for flame is lahar, to lick; to blaze; set free; a flash fire. The word is used of Israel destroying her enemies (numbers 22:4) and of the enemies of the Messiah being completely defeated and licking the dust (Psalms 72:9) it also speaks of the fire from Heaven licking up all the water upon the sacrifice offered by Elijah (1king 18:38) of the fire burning the wicked rebels In Israel (Psalms 106:8) of the flame burning up the trees (Joel 1:19) and of the hell fire punishing the wicked (Duet. 32:22).

It can be seen from these uses that Gods' ministers being a flame of fire, meaning that they are to be so full of zeal and the anointing of the spirit that nothing can stand before them. Gospel ministers are to have absolute authority and power over all works of the devil (Matthew 18:18), and represent God among men, as exemplified by Christ, the apostles and early believers.

In order to keep the lamps lit in our personal temples, should be done by the following scripture; Romans 12:1, apply this gospel doctrine to your daily routine:

"I beseech you therefore, brethren, by the mercies of God, that ye present your bodies a living sacrifice, holy, acceptable unto God, which is your reasonable service."

Paul comes to the practical application of the gospel to men. To call aside, make an appeal in view of certain facts, that ye present your bodies a living sacrifice, holy, acceptable unto God, which is your reasonable service, in other words, bring yourself to God instead of sacrifices to the altar as of the old. WE are now to be wholly God's sacrifice as were the formal sacrifices.

Not seeking the approval of men, doing things with the motive to receive recognition.

Make sure that whatever you do that it is done for the sake of Christ, this is your reasonable service and spiritual worship to present your entire body, heart and soul of intelligence to God.

This will keep us with the ample oil for the lighting of the lamps; sacrifice means to serve, obey, to offer up, oblation.

We are offering ourselves to God as a living sacrifice to be totally used of God, it will not always feel good, it will not always be comfortable, it will often be painful, but it will always be effective.

Chapter five

Bring extra oil
(Just in case)

It cost a great deal to get the anointing activated or released, that is why it is very important that you must go through the necessary process to get that oil in you released for the purpose of the mission that God has intended it for.

You must protect and value it for that intended purpose, it is very costly, so don't just give it away to anyone, let God show you how to manage it for you, after all it is His in the first place.

The ten virgins of St. Matthews 25: 1- 13, are prime examples of this, five were wise and the other five were foolish, which category would you fall in? This is how the story goes;

"Then The kingdom of heaven shall be liken to ten virgins who took their lamps and went to meet the bridegroom.

Five of them were foolish (thoughtless, without fore-thought) and five were wise (sensible, intelligent, and prudent).

For when the foolish took their lamps, they did not take (extra) oil with them;

But the wise took flasks of oil with them (also) with their lamps.

While the bridegroom lingered and was slow in coming, they all began nodding their heads, and they fell asleep.

But at midnight there was a shout, Behold, the bridegroom! Go out to meet him!

Them all those virgins got up and put their own lamps in order.

And the foolish said to the wise, give us some of your oil, for our lamps are going out.

But the wise replied, there will not be enough for us and for you; go instead to the dealers and buy for yourselves.

But while they were going away to buy, the bridegroom came, and those who were prepared went in with him to the marriage feast; and the door was shut.

Later the virgins also came and said, Lord, Lord, open (the door) to us!

But He replied, I solemnly declare to you, I do not know you (I am not acquainted with you).

Watch therefore (give strict attention and be cautious and active), for you know neither the day nor the hour when the Son of Man will come." (Ampl)

The five wise virgins came to meet the bridegroom with not only oil trimmed in their lamps, but they carried extra oil with their vessels, (just in case) "...... the wise took oil in their vessels with their lamps."

But the foolish virgins took their lamps, but carried no extra oil with them. It didn't state that they had no at all, but they did not take with them extra oil, (just in case), only what they had in their lamps. The point here is, when it was time to meet the bridegroom, after using the oil that was already in already in the lamps, while they were waiting for the bridegroom to arrive, they ran out, so they enquired of the five wise virgins to borrow some of their oil. So many of us foil to plan and prepare ahead and we often wait until the very last minute to even get started, and when the time finally comes for us to move, we find that we don't have enough time, money or material, or whatever the case may be, and we panic, so we call someone up who we know that have prepared and planned ahead, and they have plenty, and we ask to borrow from them.

I read this sign in an auto shop that reads: "The lack of preparation on your part, does not justify an emergency on my part." In so many words this is the response the five wise virgins gave to the five foolish virgins. There are times when you will have to respond like the five wise did, it is o.k. to say "NO" sometimes, their response was; "Not so, lest there be not enough for us," the wise virgins had prepared ahead of time to meet the bridegroom, they went through the process to take time to trim their lamps with oil and they even took time to fill their vessels with extra oil, just in case they would need it, a wise economist always has a back up plan for a "just in case emergency." While it may be inconvenient at the time you are preparing, it is very important to do so for what might take place outside of what you are expecting. You must continue to press while you are being pressed.

There are people around you who have the mentality like that of the five foolish virgins, who have not and will not make the necessary preparations to receive what you are receiving, but they are always pulling from you to get what they need and want. There has to come a time when you will have to inform them, "Not so, lest there be not enough for me," not to be selfish, but you cannot continue to allow people to drain you from what you have been through to get what you got for the purpose God intended it for, it will cause great delays in your assignment, and you just cannot afford fooling with foolish people, who will not press in to get it done for themselves. You must let them know on the order of the five wise to the five foolish, " Go ye rather to them that sell and buy for yourselves," in other words, we paid the price to get what we got and we can't afford the risk of missing our season, go and pay the price for yourselves. We must be careful not to just give away the anointing to anybody who are careless and unconcern. You are going through the preparation season of trimming your lamps with your processed oil, that was released from you, denying yourself. Laying aside every weight and the sin that doth so easy besets you, what it took for you, it will take for them, of course we must assist others in receiving what they need from God, you do what you are assigned to help them as God allows, but you are not assigned to go through it for them.

Chapter six

When the oil is released
(What grade is your oil?)

*W*hat happens once the necessary oil is extracted? After the extraction the remnant solid substance, called pomace, still contains a small quantity of oil. The oils extraction from the oil fruit then will be classified and graded.

Olive oil is classified by how it was produced, by its chemistry, and by its flavor. All production begins by transforming the olive fruit into olive paste. The oil is extracted by means of pressure. The several oils extracted from the olive fruit can be classified as, Virgin or refined oil:

Virgin - Means the oil was produced by the use of physical means and no chemical treatment.

Refined - Means that the oil has been chemically treated to neutralize strong tastes and neutralize the acid content (free fatty acids). Refined oil is commonly regarded as lower quality than virgin oil.

To explain my point let us go to the word of God; St. Matthew 25; 14-29, in the Amplified version.: "Watch therefore (give strict attention and be cautious and active), for you know neither the day nor hour when the Son of man shall come,

For it is like a man who was about to take a long journey and he called his servants together and entrusted them with his property.

To one he gave five talents, to another two, to another one-to each in proportion to his own personal ability. Then he departed and left the country.

He who had received the five talents went at once and traded with them, and gained five talents more.

And likewise he who had received the two talents-he also gained two talents more.

But he who received the one talent went a dug a hole in the ground and hid his master's money.

Now after a long time the master of those servants returned and settled accounts with them.

And he who had received the five talents came and brought him five talents more, saying, master, you entrusted to me five talents; see, I have gained five talents more.

His master said to him, well done, you upright (honorable, admirable) and faithful trustworthy over a little; I will put you in charge of much. Enter into and share the joy which your master enjoys.

And he also who had the two talents came forward, saying, master, you entrusted two talents to me; here I have gained two talents more.

His master said to him, well done, you upright (honorable, admirable) and faithful servant! You have been faithful and trustworthy over a little; I will put you in charge of much. Enter into and share the joy which your master enjoys.

He who received one talent also came forward, saying, master, I knew you to be a harsh and hard man, reaping where you did not sow, and gathering where you had not winnowed (the grain).

So I was afraid, and I went and hid your talent in the ground. Here you have what is your own.

But his master answered him, you wicked and lazy and idle servant! Did you indeed know that I reap where I have not sown and gather grain where I have not winnowed?

Then you should have invested my money with the bankers, and at my coming I would have received what was my own with interest.

So take the talent away from him and give it the one who has the ten talents.

For everyone who has will more be given, and he will be furnished richly so that he will have an abundance; but from the one who does not have, even what he does have will be taken away.

Jesus explains to us how to live faithfully until He comes back, we must watch and pray, work diligently and always obeying His commands and the more you are found diligently seeking His face, the more you will be found of him. Being watchful and faithful to God and not just to church or your pastor will give you increased opportunities and responsibilities. The more resources, gifts, and understanding we have, the more responsible we are to use them effectively.

God will not hold us responsible for gifts He has not given us, but He will take the gifts that He has given you, and produce oil from you, so He can get the more out of you.

The master divided the money (talents) among his servants according to their abilities and how much he could trust them. No one received more than he could handle, God promises that He won't put no more on you than you can handle. Failing to produce more for what God has require of you, is the result of laziness. The talents represent any kind of resource we are given. God gives us time, gifts, and other resources according to our abilities, and expects us to invest them wisely until He returns. God will not give you no more than you can handle, and that is predicated on how much you are willing to go through to get the best from you.

This chapter will expose who you really are and what you are made of. We have no problem being identified as great and highly anointed men and women of God, but what class of oil do you really possess and what grade is it? When God has pressed you to receive the necessary oil from you, it is not enough that oil is being released and you have an anointing on your life, that oil (your anointing) yet has to be classified, and then it must be graded, for a particular category. When the anointing is extracted from you, your first test is to see how much God can you trust with, and see if you will produce greater things for your Master with it, and you can only produce after your own kind, depending on your class category and what grade of oil you have.

THE GRADE OF THE OIL:

Quantitative analytical methods determine the oil's acidity, defined as the percent, measured by weight, of acid in it. This is a measure of the oil's chemical degradation-as the oil degrades, more fatty acids get free the glycosides, increasing the level of free acidity.

*EXTRA VIRGIN - OLIVE OIL, comes from the first pressing of the olives, contains no more than 0.8% acidity, and is judged to have superior taste. There can be no refined oil in extra - virgin olive oil.

*VIRGIN OLIVE OIL, with an acidity less than 2%, and judged to have good taste. There can be no refined oil in virgin olive oil.

*OLIVE OIL, is a blend of virgin oil, containing at most 1% acidity. It commonly lacks a strong flavor.

*OLIVE-POMACE, is a blend of refined olive-pomace oil and possibly some virgin oil. It is fit for consumption, but it may not be called olive oil. Olive-pomace is rarely found in a grocery store, it is often used for certain kinds of cooking in restaurants.

These are the grades for the oil's that I have listed, there are other grades of oil, but I wanted to highlight these, to help make my point to you.

When you buy olive oil in the store, and the label reads 100% pure olive oil, sounds like a high end product, doesn't it? But in fact is often the lowest quality available.

This is what we often deal with in the church world, a lot of people with labels that read, 100% pure, and the effect of the contents is only good for one purpose, this oil is usually only good for baking or frying.

When the oil is being released from you, don't just settle for that and base your destiny there, keep going back to the crushing place, which is on your knees, so that God can get more out of you and to get better quality from you. We don't need to only trust in Him, but He also need to trust us with what He has given us, so that we can produce more.

In St. Luke 12:48, we read, "But he who did not know and did things worthy of a beating shall be beaten with few (lashes). For everyone to whom much is given, of him shall much be required; and of him to whom men entrust much, they will require and demand more."

If you want more from God, He will demand more from you.

As I travel and minister Gods' word and release His love and anointing, people often ask me, "what is the secret of that anointing on you, I have never seen an anointing so rich before," I can only respond, "I let God press it out of me," the bible says, to let your light so shine so men can see, it didn't read, make it shine, all we need to do is stay on our

face before God, until the oil is released for your next assignment, each assignment needs a release of oil supply from
you, and when it is released make sure it is what God need
to complete the assignment effectively. I remember when the
Lord spoke to me one day and said, when you go abroad to
minister my word, I want you to first release my love to my
people and the anointing would flow freely from there, ever
since then, it has been easy to minister.

When I was in the hospital recently, the doctor came to
my bed and asked me if he could pray for me before they
treated me, of course I said yes, realizing that this was God's
doing, His prayer was (as my wife and sister witnessed)
"Lord God, please guide us on how to treat this man of God,
to prepare him for his next assignment," I will give you
details of this testimony in chapter 9, but God was prepping
me for my next assignment.

Get ready to go through all the way, the world need you
to come out with the highest quality in anointing, when the
"oil is released."

Chapter seven

My crushing place
(My testimony)

*W*herefore do I take my flesh in my teeth, and put my life in mine own hand? Job 13:14.The idea here seems to be that Job was in such misery that he even bit his own flesh to ease the pain that he was suffering; or this could be a proverb about taking his life in his own hands. Although Job suffered to the point of possibly wanting to end his own life, his confidence remained in his God. "Though he slay me, yet will I trust in him: but I will maintain my own ways before him." Job 13:15, Job was determined to trust in God and maintain his own ways before him, regardless of the outcome, Job thought his ways was righteous, so God found it necessary to crush Job by afflicting him, but after all that Job went through, he maintains his integrity.

To begin with I would like to take you to the place of my youth and go from there; as my mother told me and my older siblings verify. The enemy made several attempts to kill me, when I was just a toddler, at the age of two or three years old, as it was told me, I was running around being a typical toddler, running through the house getting into what I could get into, my mother was supposedly doing some baking, and the entire stove she had at the time would get extremely hot, and I ran up to the stove and put both of my hands on the stove, my hands began to burn and get stuck on the stove, I scream as a toddler would under these circumstances, one of my older siblings ran to my aide and released me from the stove, by this time my mother runs in and begin to pray and anoint my hands with blessed oil, my hands was quickly blistering and swelling, my mother rushes me to the hospital and the doctor treats me, the doctor tells my mother that it was third degree burns and he don't understand why I haven't lost my hands, he says that God evidently has use for these hands. Today I bear the scars from my youth, both of the palms of my hands are scarred, Lamentations 3:27, says, It is good for a man that he bear the yoke (servitude) in his youth. It is recorded up to this point and witnessed by many, that God has used these hands to perform countless miracles and three people have been raised from the dead.

Our late beloved mother, Gladys Marie Prichett, was a faithful, dedicated and praying woman of God, she faithfully prayed for all eleven of her children, she would speak into everyone of our lives and let us know what God is going to use us for if we would serve him faithfully, everyone of us received his/her own impartation from her ministry. She would always tell me that I couldn't make my own plans for my life, that God has already planned it for me, she would tell that God was going to use you for the world, I could not understand it at the time, but it always remained in my spirit, I thought that if God was going to use me for the world, that I was to get special treatment from everyone, well, little did I know that the enemy had some plans for me as well, plans and plots to destroy and assassinate me, But God would always prove to me each time that his hand was on me to bring me out.

This one particular time, when I was riding my bike in this field by this canal a few streets from our house, there are signs clearly posted around this canal that says, "Stay out, Stay alive," but I was going towards the canal at a very high rate of speed, being a daring twelve year old, I don't know what I was thinking, but as I was approaching the canal, the front of the tire hits this stick that was sticking out of the ground, and this causes the bike to begin to flip me over into the canal, these canal's have claimed several lives when people would try to swim or fall in, the water is deep and shallow, I just knew I was going in the canal and not coming out alive, when all of a sudden, I felt something jerk me and my bike from behind back to the ground, after catching my breath, I looked around to see who was it that saved my life, there was no one around in sight, I ran home to share this with my mother, who told me that my angel saved me from going into that canal, she also explained to me that the enemy was the one who would drive me to the canal, but God spared my life.

Moses even as a baby, his life was threatened by an enemy, during the very time of his birth, the Pharoah orders all Hebrew male babies to be thrown into the Nile river, but God instructs Moses' mother to hide Moses by making him a basket made out of pitch, to place him in, to defy the enemy in his attempt to kill Moses, the very river Pharoah is throwing the Hebrew male babies in, God directs Moses' mother to put the basket that she put Moses in, to send it down that very Nile river, while she watches over it.

When God has a plan for your life, and while he is preparing you, at the same time he is protecting you, God will sometimes put you in the very line of your enemy, but your enemy won't be able to find you he can't recognize you, because God has hidden you from your enemy. There are times when your enemy is in hot pursuit of you, and he can't find you to carry out his plans to kill you, because God has put you in hiding, so that he won't recognize you when you go by him. These are probably the days when you are experiencing the most vulnerable and lonelier than ever, but God deemed it necessary to hide you for a season, even while you are in the direct line of the enemy. This is an indicator to you that you belong to God and can nothing pluck you out of his hand, but this is God's way of processing you and me for His purpose, by using the enemy to afflict you, crush, and press you out, so God can get the Glory out of us, what the devil means for evil, God turns it around for our good.

I remember one early morning while I was on one of my prayer walks, declaring things in my city, while in the middle of the walk at about 3:30 a.m. I spotted this car following me, I am always aware of my surroundings, there was about four young men in this car and as they were passing in a slow rate of speed, I could hear one young man speak, and say and I quote, "where did he go? I don't see him, I can't shoot him he's gone," then they circle around two more times, then finally left, while this was taking place, I was praying, "Lord, hide me in your pavilion," this is why it is very important that during your season of being hidden away, that we don't rush out of hiding before time.

At about age fifteen, the beginning of some very dark days ahead, by this time I am experiencing feelings of rejection, the enemy's plans are in effect to destroy my life. He begins to play with my mind to tell me that I am a failure, that nobody wanted me around, the few friends that I did have seem to be pulling away from me, this goes on to lead up to suicide attempts, on several occasions, I attempted to over dose on pills that I could find in the medicine cabinet, they would rush me to the hospital to get my stomach pumped, on one occasion as I taken a whole bottle of pills, it looked like this wasn't working fast enough, so I swallowed a whole bottle of rubbing alcohol, until I found myself waking up in the emergency room again, my mother spoke the word of God over me, and I could hear the words very clear, "the thief cometh not, but to steal, and to kill, and to destroy: I am come that they might have life, and that they might have it more abundantly," St. John 10:10, the enemy is a thief, and he comes in subtle forms to gain access, but God is there waiting on him, to remind the thief, that he/she has abundant life, you can't take this one.

I continue to experience more rejection, although everyone who really don't know me considers me to be the good, sweet innocent Garvin, in all actuality it was becoming dark and lonely inside, I felt I was without hope for a bright future, I remember asking myself on several occasions, what would ever become of me? What really is my purpose on this earth? So I start to find my own happiness in the world of sin.

Our family grew up in the black part of Bakersfield, California, it is considered a portion of east Bakersfield, and the popular place at that time to go to have a good time, was a place called the Elk's club, that is where all the black people would go to party as well as neighborhood parties, I chose not to be apart of that scene, you see I still had to keep up this good boy image everyone expects from me. When the neighbors would see me walking to the bus stop, in my nice slacks and starched ironed shirts, they assumed that I was either going to work or to school somewhere, in all actuality I was going across town to do my thing, and I would often end up in this bar called, The Silver Fox, where people did not know me, there I would get drunk and end up in a hotel somewhere, with two or three women, I became very promiscuous, things got so bad, the enemy begin to invade my mind, I couldn't sleep at night, I would run down the street in the middle of the night trying to out run words, that he would crowd my mind with, I would often wake up in cars where I had slept for the night, sometimes in junk yards. The enemy would start demanding me to do things I had no desire to do, but under his control I would end up doing just what he wanted me to do, I would get drunk, get high on weed, pass out and wake up on the streets, depressed and all messed up.

The enemy had engulfed my mind so bad, that I could not control my thoughts any longer, after awhile, I couldn't control my life. Many times I would pass out without warning, and I would end up in the emergency rooms time after time, they would hook me up to brain scans to see if something was going on, they could not find anything, but the doctor would tell my mother, if he continues to have these episodes, he is going to lose his mind and eventually die, I remember my mother saying to me, "not so, God has a plan for your life, you will not lose your mind, God is going to use you for the world," she was speaking those things that be not as though they were.

One day while I was waiting on the bus for school, I heard the enemy tell me that I was going to die that day, and right away, he attacked my mind, the only way to explain what happens next is like this; while I was passing out, I could hear and see a bunch of pigs in my mind getting louder and louder with squeaking sounds, then the pigs would start yelling at me, but I couldn't understand what they were saying, after awhile I would hear someone say, "I think we lost him, there is no pulse," the next things I know I am standing in a beautiful garden, in front of someone in a white robe, I couldn't see his face, the only thing he did was sit on this beautiful white bench, then I remember waking up in the emergency room. I can't quite explain who this was that I stood before in that garden, but for sure I do know that I left this earth for awhile. From that experience I made up my mind to get my life right with God because things just wasn't getting any better with me but only worst, now people are starting to really distance themselves from me because I am now being labeled as being crazy and cursed, because of these episodes I keep having.

I am about to turn 18, and I was planning a big party, to celebrate turning 18, but my mother invites me to a revival service, with this powerful evangelist from Los Angeles who was the speaker, her name was Evangelist Colts, I agreed to go, it was the night before my 18th birthday, the next night I plan to really party, but when I attended this service, Evangelist Colts was preaching a very powerful and convincing hell fire message, she just repeated over and over, "if you don't get saved before it's to late then you're going to hell," and during this it seemed that she was speaking directly to me, my heart was convicted until before I knew it I was on the altar, and the altar workers got a hold to me, and begin casting out unclean spirits out of me, this was the beginning of God setting me free. Pastor Charlotte Davis who was also my aunt, and a very powerful woman of God, she started calling out the names of these unclean spirits that I was possessed with, and the mothers that was working on the altar surrounded me, they did not let me go until I was set free. Even though I am delivered from all these unclean spirits, I was still dealing with other challenges during the development of my saved life, but God always brings me through victoriously.

God takes me through a series of crushing process, to prepare me for what he is assigning me to do now, today I am a founding pastor of a church now for eight years at this writing, a membership of about six hundred and I oversee now 20 churches in the states and in Jamaica and growing rapidly, but before I got to this point I went through a season of crushing to get the oil for this assignment; I was serving in a ministry at that time it had been three years and the Lord spoke to me to tell me that he was sending me to start a great work for his glory, and that it was going to be a great impact, oh yes I was thinking that the impact would be that people would be coming from all over Bakersfield and be blessed because of the ministry, although that happened to some degree, the impact was from the enemy to fight against us, the ministry and my family, attacks came from every-where to attempt to frustrate our purpose, no one person is to blame for what we went through, it was God's way of crushing me for this purpose, he had to get all the pulpy mass out of me to make sure that he received fresh clear and pure oil from me, even though I had to fight to stay in the race, but my fight had to be right. Many times during the course of this particular season, I experienced so much stress, I would go to the restroom, I would release a tremendous amount of blood, I become very lonely and yes depressed, on several occasions I attempted to give up the ministry and live a normal life, feeling at times that this wasn't worth going through and taking my family through, but then God would always remind me that although everyone who came to the ministry he did not send, but there were those who was sent by him to receive their healing and deliverance, and if I were to throw in the towel now, what do I think would happen to them; this would always give me the courage to go back and fight. During the process of building this ministry, we went through at least three major splits, this can be and was very discouraging and disappointing and makes you wonder did you really hear from God, but God would always encourage me and remind me that we were experiencing a season of crushing in most of the cases, don't get me wrong in some of the cases it was because of major mistakes and bad decisions on my part that caused some of the splits, but I knew the importance of repenting and not to makes the same mistakes over again, I had to learn from those mistakes and bad deci-sions, and during these seasons I learned to become more compassionate and tender regarding Gods' precious people, this is why we must complete the full process of our crushing seasons, for the purpose to get all of us out of us, God don't need us for the assignments, just our vessels.

I have many more testimony's to share with you, but I am going to give you one more. I had many encounters with angels in my lifetime, this particular time was when we first moved back to Bakersfield from Palm Springs, California about eleven years ago. We were living with my sister whom we call "Shane," we were having car trouble and I really didn't have any money to have it fixed, all I had was twenty two dollars to my name, keep in mind I had two ten dollar bills and two one dollar bills, but I called the mechanic shop anyway and explained my situation to them, they said to bring the car in that normally it would cost much more to replace the part, but they could bypass something and we would have to do without running heat in the car, but as long as the car was in driving condition was important, so I took the chance to drive the car across town, and I made it to the shop without the car running hot, in about a couple of hours, they inform me that the car is ready and my bill was exactly twenty two dollars, thank God, because that is all I had, but this wasn't the miracle, on my way home I had the mind to stop at this particular thrift store downtown, and while I am looking around in this store, these two gentlemen approach me and immediately began to speak, "God bless you man of God," and while he is speaking, he pulls out his wallet and takes out some money and hands it to me and says, "God did not mean for you pay anything to get your car fixed," I immediately counted the money and it was two ten dollar bills and two one dollar bills, right then and there I began to praise God, these men continue to minister to me, they mentioned my wife by name and said that she had been crying and that God was going dry her tears, they told that God heard my prayers and promises to take care of my family, and he has been doing that, he concluded by saying, "those that bless you will be blessed, and those that curse you will be cursed, and they exited out of the building swiftly and I followed behind them to see if my suspicions were right that they were angels, after all they looked like normal human beings, there was nothing extra ordinary about their appearance, as I looked outside and I went around the corners, they were nowhere in sight, I came to the conclusion that they were angels sent by God, how else can you explain this, well I was both excited and nervous at the same time, almost to excited to drive, but I managed to make it to my sister's apartment, and when my wife sees me, she says to me that it looked as though I saw a ghost, I replied, better, I had an encounter with angels, I told her all about it and I showed her the money and let her know that the car is fixed, we both rejoiced. Here is the rest of the story, no it's not over yet, a few hours pass when we get a knock at the door, it was this man of God, who was a member of the church I was attending, he appeared very nervous, and he handed me some money in my hand, and began to explain his reason for being there, he said that he and his family was on the beach, when God spoke to him and said didn't I tell you to give the man of God some money to pay for his car to get fixed, the Lord told him to leave the beach now and get that money to him, I counted the money, yes, it was two ten dollar bills and two one dollar bills.

God will take care of your business if you will take care of his business, he has proven himself to me time after time, that he is with me and he will not forsake me and he will do the same for you if you will live for him, trust in him and obey his commands, don't compromise anything that he told you to do or what he is taking you through for the assignment he has you on.

Chapter eight

The deeper call

$\mathcal{A}$s the hart panteth after the water brooks, so panteth my soul after thee, O God.

My soul thirsteth for God, for the living God: when shall I come and appear before God?

My tears have been my meat day and night, while they continually say unto me, where is thy God?

When I remember these things, I pour out my soul in me: for I had gone with the multitude, I went with them to the house of God, with the voice of joy and praise, with a multitude that kept holyday.

Why art thou cast down, O my soul? And why art thou disquieted in me? Hope thou in God: for I shall praise him for the help of his countenance.

O my God, my soul is cast down within me: therefore will I remember thee from the land of Jordan, and of the Hermonites, from the hill Mizar.

Deep calleth unto deep at the noise of thy waterspouts: all thy waves and thy billows are gone over me. Psalms 42: 1-7 (KJV)

This Psalm was perhaps written by David himself on the occasion of his flight from his son Absolom, (2nd Samuel 17:24), then David came to Mahanaim. And Absolom passed over Jordan, he had all the men of Israel with him.

Having crossed the fords of Jordan near Jericho and landing on the eastern heights, taking refuge in Mahanaim, a place of refuge before, for Jacob, now for David.

David on the run from his son and those that pursued him, seeks refuge in the presence of God. While David was being pursued, he was in pursuit of God, believe it or not this is where God wants us, while those who oppose you and are pursuing you to fight against you, the idea here is to get you to pursue God in a realm of a deeper call.

Psalms 42:1 says, as the Hart panteth after the water brooks, so panteth my soul after thee, O God.

After a weary, yet a victorious life saving run, the hart instinctively seeks after the river. David banned from the public worship, was lonely and homesick for the Lord his God, (the living God) his deepest heart had an insatiable desire for the presence of God.

David longed for the temple of God (physical) where he openly worshipped God, but God wanted to bring him from the comfortable place where he was used to worshipping God religiously and to call him to a deeper relationship in worship intimately.

This is the call God is attempting to get us to answer, when we face certain troubles in the life of our ministries. Even though David was anointed to be king over the nation of Israel, God allowed trouble to pursue him, to attempt to get him to answer the call for a DEEPER relationship with Him. David's banishment from the house of God did not make him to be indifferent, on the contrary, it intensified his desire to commune with God.

David said in Psalms 42:3, "my tears have been my meat day and night, while they continually say unto me, where is your God? In reference to this scripture, let us go to Psalms

126:5, they that sow in tears shall reap in joy. David only had an appetite for his tears, because of the loneliness and hunger pains, the hunger for the presence of God and the only thing at this point to satisfy his hunger was his tears, day and night, with no one to talk to and cry on their shoulders. Sometimes all we have to satisfy our spiritual hunger pains are our tears, often we only have our tears to sow, we had to evacuate, had to run and leave everything behind. Psalms 126: 5, says, they that sow in tears shall reap in joy, it will soon be reaping season for you, if you faint not.

While David was praying of his distress and appeal to God, God answers him in the place where he is located now. He says in Psalms 42: 7, "Deep calleth unto deep at the noise of the waterspouts; all the waves and thy billows are gone over me," wave after wave of the troubled seas had swallowed him up, yet he knew where to find hope from that point.

Before you reach the next level in God, you first must go through a realm of the deep in worship to Him, before he will take you up, you first must be abased.

Once David reached the deep and of the depth of his season of trouble, his level of worship changed, Psalms 42: 11, asks, "why art thou cast down, O my soul, and why art thou disquieted in me?" at this point, it didn't matter that God wasn't responding to David's appeal, still David worships,…. "hope thou in God: for I shall yet praise him, who is the help of thy countenance," in other words, despite of my enemy pursuing me, I know, you are my salvation and safe haven, you're the salvation of my countenance.

In my many distresses during my walk with God, he allowed me to search for him more so than try to search for answers as to why I was facing such troubles, when wave after wave of the troubled seas had swallowed me up, I learned to listen for God's voice and when I heard it, I answered it, while I was in deep trouble, I answered the deep call of God, and now know matter what I face in times of trouble it is not to deep that I can't hear God's call.

Chapter nine

A walk through the dark valley

*I*n the process of writing this testimonial book, I often ran into obstacles that kept hindering me to go forward with this project, as I would get the inspiration to write and I would start flowing, there was something that would happen that needed my full attention and I had to stop for a period from writing, and I would lose the inspiration to continue, this process would repeat itself time after time, and each period it would take me months to even regain the inspiration to start back writing, then when it looked like I would finish the book and have the manuscript ready for the publishers, a major attack on me and my wife's physical bodies took place, while I was in the hospital in the intensive care unit, the Lord speaks to my spirit to inform me, you could not complete the book until you lived through the final chapter and then write it, he said I must walk you and your wife through the valley of the shadow of death, and bring you out on the other side with the victory.

Psalms 23 is a very familiar passage of scripture text for most Christians, but do we really know the Lord as being a caring shepherd and a dependable guide, are we willing to follow him and obey his commands. He is our only hope for eternal life and hope for divine security.

This Psalm of David tells us that, "The Lord is my shepherd; I shall not want.

He maketh me lie down in green pastures: he leadeth me besides the still waters.

He restoreth my soul: he leadeth me in the path of righteousness for his name's sake.

Yea, though I walk through the valley of the shadow of death, I will fear no evil: for thou art with me; thy rod and thy staff they comfort me.

Thou prepares a table before me in the presence of mine enemies: thou anointest my head with oil; my cup runneth over.

Surely goodness and mercy shall follow me all the days of my life: and I will dwell in the house of the Lord for ever.

In describing the Lord as a shepherd, David wrote out of his own experience, because he had spent his early years caring for sheep (1 Samuel 16: 10, 11).

Sheep are completely dependant on the shepherd for provision, guidance, and protection. The New Testament calls Jesus the Good Shepherd (John 10:11); the Great Shepherd (Hebrews 13:20,21); and the Chief Shepherd (1Peter 5:4).

As the Lord is the Good shepherd, so we are the sheep, not dumb, frightened, passive animals, but obedient followers wise enough to follow one who will lead us in the right places and in right ways. The Psalm does not focus on the animal like qualities of sheep, but on the discipleship qualities of those who follow.

When we allow God, our shepherd, to guide us, we have contentment. When we chose to sin, however, we go our own way and cannot blame God for the environment we create for ourselves. Our shepherd knows the green pastures and still waters that will restore us. We will reach these places only by following him obediently.

Death casts a frightening shadow over us because we are entirely helpless in its presence. We can struggle with other enemies, pain, suffering, disease, injury, only one can walk us through death's dark valley and bring us safely on the other side, God almighty, our shepherd.

At the end of 2005, around Christmas time, my wife, Connie ended up in the hospital, prior to going to the hospital she already had a scheduled surgery, but there were other complications going on here so she had to go in the hospital, to get this taken care of, they had to administer blood transfusion, and they released her, they could not do the surgery due to these complications, we had to bring her home, Connie is a very powerful dynamic woman of God, very active and full of strength and vitality, but she had become too weak to do what she use to do, so we began to seek God for answers, then while waiting and praying for answers for Connie's physical situation, the enemy attacks my body, I started experiencing weakness, losing weight, and other symptoms in my body was causing great concern, I was getting weaker by the day, Connie begin to express what she thought what was wrong with me, I replied that although I don't deny that these symptoms exist, they don't have the right to exist in me.

On January seventh, I was scheduled to fly to North Carolina and Florida, for ministry, for eight days, four days in each state, my wife was trying to encourage me to see the doctor about what was going on in my body, I knew I had to be on this trip, for the assignment at hand, I did realize that if I went to the doctor then that I would not be on the plane on January the seventh, things started transpiring in my body, about two weeks prior, so I made up in my mind that I was going on this trip. My son in the gospel was traveling with me, Bishop Gary Washington from Oakland, California, so we fly to North Carolina first, spend four days there, then fly to Florida, by then I am getting worst than ever, I even pass out in my suite, I don't know how long I was out, but I wake up, and continues my assignment for the Lord, while in Florida, we travel to a city to minister to one of my other son's in the gospel, Minister Marcus Murchinson, when we were leaving to go back to the city where we were staying, Minister Murchinson, says to us, that while we were praying for him, he saw a vision of blood covering Bishop Washington's entire head, and blood covering my entire body, he admits that he didn't know what it meant, I thought I did, but I would later find out. We finally land back in California, and by now I'm almost to weak to walk, I am very dehydrated, I still had two hours to get to Bakersfield, and once I arrive, my wife tells me that I need to go to emergency, I asked her if I could sleep in my own bed, for the night and I would go in the morning, while I was sleeping my wife shakes me to wake me up she said that I was sleeping to sound and to still, so I finally agree to go to the emergency, once they saw me, they inform me that the blood sugar in my body was over seven hundred and the blood pressure was extremely high, I had never been diagnosed with diabetes before even though my mother was. They immediately treats me in E.R. and when they learned that I was like this for three weeks, they rushed me to the Intensive Care Unit, but before I go, a doctor comes in to see me and tells me that I was in good hands, he explains that he was a Christian, and he asked could he pray for me? Of course I said yes, this was his prayer, "Lord, lead and guide us on how to treat this man of God, so we can prepare him for his next assignment," from there on God was manifesting himself to us that he was with me.

Thy rod and thy staff they comfort me - the rod and staff are symbols of the shepherd's office, by them he guides the sheep. When passing through the shadowy ravine, the sheep know that the gentle tap of the shepherd's crook or of his rod is designed for their safe passage. In the Intensive care Unit, they work hard to find out what organs are damaged and how bad, I just lay there all alone in the quiet stillness of this place, I could even vision the darkness of the valley I was walking through, it was lonely and cold, but God would give me a strong peace in my spirit, the Lord reminded me that he had angels watching over me, then I received a note from the nurse that Bishop Washington called and sent a note to tell me that he saw two angels standing on both sides of my bed, I knew without a doubt that I was not alone, where my room was located, allowed me to be totally isolated, and they kept my door closed so I wouldn't be disturbed by anyone, and allowed me to hear not in a realm I never heard before, well a couple of times I heard voices, and once or twice I could understand what was said, one time I heard a voice say "the nurse in coming let's get ready," and right then the nurse enters my room, and on another occasion, I heard a voice say, "the doctor is on his way," and after awhile he walks in my room, I believe I heard the angels talking and I believe they were my rod and staff, which also represents protection and guidance. One night the doctor came in my room, and he asked me if anyone ever told me that my heart was enlarging itself, I replied, my father died of it, he then tells me that the next day I was going for a lot of testing for most of the day, mainly to look at my heart, after he leaves I begin to question God, and I asked him why is this happening? I thought you promised me that the generational curses from my family was broken, he responded, "the curses had to hit you first, then become broken as a sign that it is done," he then said, "I will get the glory out of this." The next day as they roll me in for testing the Lord reminds me to look at the blood that was covering me that the man of God was referring to when he saw, Bishop Washington's head covered with it, and your body covered with it, now I knew what it all meant, Bishop Washington had been going through some heavy trials that caused a lot frustration and confusion and God promise to cover him through this, and in my case, he was covering my body through what I was facing. While they were preparing me for these procedures, I could literally see thousands specks of blood all over, and during the procedures, I was singing blood songs, "O it was the Blood for me!" and when they were done with all of the procedures, one of the technicians, said to me, "I don't know what their doing with you in I.C.U., but as far as I'm concern, you can do what you've been doing before, you have no limitations," I didn't catch it right away, and when I got back in my room, I begin to pray and ask God, to make sure everything is find with the tests, he said to me, "the technician has already given you a preliminary report," I started praising God at that point, when the doctor saw me the next time, he asked me if I wanted to go home that night or in the morning? I said, tonight of course, he then said all of your tests were negative, you are a mystery to us.

I am coming out on the other side of the valley of the shadow of death with the victory.

Two weeks later, the blood sugar is under control, and I am not taking as much medicine as I was when I was in the hospital, God is even clearing up the diabetes. Then one early Friday morning, Connie wakes me up in extreme pain, I rushes her to the emergency, they admit her, her blood is low again and she has pneumonia, they begin tests to try to locate where she is bleeding, to cause her blood to stay as low as it has been, she has been in the hospital now at this writing for two weeks, and every test that they have ran so far, they have not found anything, I know that God is with her through this dark valley, she will come out on the other side with the victory.

If by any chance you are experiencing going through a death valley walk, make sure you are walking with God, and you will fear no evil.

Printed in the United States
50899LVS00002B/1-441